ON COMING ALIVE
JOURNALING THROUGH GRIEF

Written by
Lexi Behrndt

This jounral is in memory of

_____

INTRODUCTION

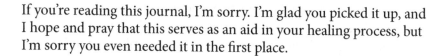

If you're reading this journal, I'm sorry. I'm glad you picked it up, and I hope and pray that this serves as an aid in your healing process, but I'm sorry you even needed it in the first place.

Here are the first things I want to tell you: I see you. I feel for you. I get you in a way I wish I didn't. I am so sorry for your pain.

And here are the second: You are not alone. And there is always hope.

I don't know your exact circumstance. I don't know your exact hurt. I can't, and I never could. Even if you were to tell me every story and every hurt and place me in your shoes for moments at a time, I still couldn't fully know or understand. But I do know pain. I know the awkward jumble that it turns life into, and I know the weaving in and out of despair and normalcy that occur within your every day and sometimes, your every hour.

I know life hasn't been fair to you. I know it's been hard. I know you feel crumbly and shattered, and all the edges still feel very sharp. I know it's hard for other to understand.

I know it feels impossible to meet the expectations and demands of life at a time when your heart is laid waste. Don't let anyone rush you through your pain. There's a balance of grief and healing, of joy and brokenness, and you have to move through both to make your rough edges smooth again. You have to wade through the thick waters to heal your broken pieces, and it will happen— gradually, steadily, sometimes with setbacks, but you'll slowly mend.

I know there is pressure to be more, but please don't plaster on smiles. Please don't just say the right words, go through all the right steps, letting the world choreograph your life. Please don't be afraid to be honest. Please don't cover up the hurt and suffer— quietly, silently. That's not the way to mend. Healing doesn't happen under a facade, and you've been through too much to have to fake it.

I know you feel weak, but remember that there is beauty in the brokenness. When you are reduced to nothing but soul, you radiate an extraordinary power. When you experience searing loss and your heart continues beating, there is strength in that. When pain whispers the hurtful lies and giving up and succumbing sounds like the best plan, find that strength, find that hope that is greater and that love that is deeper than any amount of pain, then cling to it, and don't you dare let go.

I know you feel isolated. Pain does that, but remember you are not alone. There's not a struggle or fight you could face that hasn't been fought before. There's not a challenge or fear or tragedy known to man that could ever make you completely alone. Even when you don't feel it, there are bands and tribes full of broken people, suffering, aloud or silently right alongside you. All you have to do is use your little voice and make it big by being honest. Make it brave by crying out for help. Make it powerful by sharing the truth and owning it in its full capacity and saying to someone: "Help." or "This is my mess." or "I need you."

I need you to do this, because I need you to promise me that you won't live this pain alone.

The truth is, we're all a little broken. But when we share love and hope together, raising our voices in honesty and bravery, we can all mend, piece by piece, and we can all be a little more whole.

You're a little broken. I'm a little broken. I see you. I feel for you. I get you in a way I wish I didn't.

Remember, friend, you're not alone. I'm so thankful to join hands with you on this journey of coming alive again in some small way.

A friend who knows
Lexi

Prompt 1:

WHAT WE MEAN WHEN WE SAY "COMING ALIVE"

We're all broken in our own ways. We all suffer in our own ways. We all will lose someone we love, sometime, to something. We all will face some sort of heartache in our lives. That's just the way the world works... We all will wake up one day and find ourselves in some sort of darkness. The darkness has a place, and the darkness is necessary to navigate through as we grieve. The darkness is nothing to be afraid of, though it be uncomfortable and a little (or a lot) dismal, but hear me out on this: I don't believe we are meant to stay there permanently. I don't believe that we're meant to spend the rest of our lives faking it just to survive and get through. As a friend put it, I don't believe we are meant to sleepwalk through our lives, numbing ourselves to all the pain and the joy. We were meant to come alive, still feeling pain, still living with part of ourselves missing or scarred, but also feeling joy, love, happiness, peace, fulfillment. That's the thing about coming alive. You feel it all, no longer numb, embracing life and embracing living. It is possible. You don't have to find yourself years down the road only half alive, still shielding yourself from the pain. Grief is unique for everyone and everyone has their own timetable. There is nothing wrong with that, but know that there is hope, and that one day, you can open your eyes, and see a tiny glimmer in the dark and reach out for it. And when you grab hold, your eyes might adjust, and you might find another patch of light. There is more. And there is light. Still, the light shines, even when you haven't seen it in a very long time. There is joy (even if all you can currently find is laughing aloud at my suggestion of it). There is mending, and there is a heart that holds more love than an unbroken heart can fathom. Grief and love spill out of the broken heart, and in time, you might see what a beautiful thing that is. Life can suck. Really suck. Losses are not fair, ever. Heartache rips away at everyone with no discrimination. And even in the madness that sometimes we can find in life, there still is a reason to look for the light, and when we find it, to pull one another toward it. Let us pull you. Where are

●●●

you at this starting ground?

_____

_____

_____

_____

_____

_____

_____

_____

_____

_____

_____

_____

_____

_____

_____

_____

_____

_____

•●•

•••

•••

Prompt 2:

SACRED LOVE

"In all this world, there is no love for you like mine."
-Maya Angelou

The love possessed in your heart for your loved one is a force to behold. It's stronger than the grasp of death; it's greater than a sea of tears. Your love is powerful. Your love is great. Grief is the way that love is manifesting itself in your heart for the one who is no longer physically present. Grief can be dark and isolating and painful, but remember that love is the reason you are in this place. Love is what brought you here. Love is what you still hold in your heart. A love that is still shared though worlds may separate you. This love. Spend some time reflecting on this love today. Soak in the beauty of it. What does it look like? What represents this love to you? What are ways you can continue to pour out your love for your loved one, even though they are no longer physically present?

_____

_____

_____

_____

_____

_____

_____

●●●

•••

•••

•••

Prompt 3:

SHATTERED DREAMS

"She felt as if the mosaic she had been assembling out of life's little shards got dumped to the ground, and there was no way to put it back together."
-Anne Lamott

It's hard to say how you got here. You're not even quite sure how your life unraveled and you found yourself sitting in a pile of tissues, broken wishes, and dreams. Your plans were big. Your hopes were perfect, but one thing led to another, and like an unstable tower, it all came crashing down. This wasn't the plan, that's for sure. And now, you're not quite sure where to go. You're not quite sure who you are anymore, let alone why you're still here. How could you have to keep walking and moving and breathing when your world— all your dreams, the best-made plans— have shattered? I'm so sorry you're here, that you're hurting, that life hasn't been kind. This world can be a cruel place and you've borne the brunt of that truth. When you lose someone you love, it takes a part of you. You ache for them, the irreplaceable spot they fit into within your heart longs for their physical presence, but somehow, somewhere along the way, something happened, and they are no longer next to you. I'm so sorry for that. So, so sorry. You need to hear this: it's okay to acknowledge your shattered dreams. It's okay to ache for them. It's okay to feel like your whole world has come crashing down. It's important to sit in these feelings, to move through them. Today, do just that. Spill the broken pieces of your heart onto this page, and move through the pain knowing that the reason you are here is because of the love.

●●●

•••

•••

•••

•••

Prompt 4:

TINY PATCHES OF LIGHT

"Hope is being able to see that there is light despite all the darkness."
-Desmond Tutu

Darkness can drape over our days like a veil. Grief brings darkness, and the quest of this journal is to guide us as we search, hand-in-hand for the light together. What does the darkness feel like to you? What are the tiny patches of light you can cling to in the midst of it? It could be the scent of your favorite flower, a smile from someone you love, a dish of your favorite food, or the way the sunset is painted across the sky. What are your patches of light? Find them and don't let them go.

_____

_____

_____

_____

_____

_____

_____

_____

●●●

•••

•••

•••

Prompt 5:

ASKING QUESTIONS

"It's not that I'm so smart, it's just that I stay with problems longer."
-Albert Einstein

It's normal to ask questions, to wonder "why?" and "how?", and to cry out in anger and frustration. In the space below, share your questions, even your hardest ones. Though in this lifetime we may never find the answers, it's important to wrestle through them rather than shoving them aside. Identify one place you can go to seek answers, or at the very least— peace in the midst of your questions.

_____

_____

_____

_____

_____

_____

_____

_____

•••

•••

•••

•••

Prompt 6:

LOVE LETTER TO THEM

"I love you with my soul because my soul never stops or forgets."
- Rumi

Write a letter to your loved one below. What do you miss about them? How does their absence feel? How are they inspiring you and pushing you toward love and life? What can you do to honor them?

_____

_____

_____

_____

_____

_____

_____

_____

_____

_____

●●●

••

•••

•••

Prompt 7:

SHOCK

How could I possibly be here? How could this have happened to me? To them? How? Why? Shock is normal. Feeling numb is normal; it's nearly a partner with grief in the early days, almost giving our broken hearts space to beat, because if they felt the full brunt of pain, it would crush them. Shock. Numbness. These feelings can be helpful, but it's also important to gently part the curtains every now and then, to see beyond the initial pain, to tap into what is happening in your heart. Today, tap into that. Are you experiencing shock? Numbness? Pain? What things still feel unreal to you? What do you see when you part the curtain?

_____

_____

_____

_____

_____

_____

_____

•●•

•••

•••

•••

Prompt 8:

THE HARD PLACES

"We've got to live, no matter how many skies have fallen."
-D.H. Lawrence

Complete this prompt today: "The moment I will never forget…"

_____

_____

_____

_____

_____

_____

_____

_____

_____

_____

_____

_____

_____

•••

•••

●●●

•••

Prompt 9:

SEARCHING FOR STARS

"Though my soul may set in darkness, it will rise in perfect light;
I have loved the stars too fondly to be fearful of the night."
-Sarah Williams

What are the stars around you? What do you love about your life? List at least twenty things below.

_____

_____

_____

_____

_____

_____

_____

_____

_____

_____

_____

•••

‹‹‹

•••

Prompt 10:

EMPTY

"Your absence has gone through me like thread through a needle.
Everything I do is stitched with its color."
-W.S. Merwin

Emptiness. That's often how loss feels. Emptiness because there was a spot that they once filled, and in their physical absence, it feels like a black hole. It's easy to take that emptiness and force other things into its place: numbing agents like alcohol, food or throwing yourself into exercise, work, or relationships. But maybe the healthiest thing you can do is to honor that emptiness and to fill it with the love. What does that empty place look like? What have you been trying to fill it with? How can you fill it with the love you still share?

_____

_____

_____

_____

_____

_____

_____

•••

•••

•••

●●●

Prompt 11:

WHEN GOOD SEEMS IMPOSSIBLE

"Even the darkest night will end and the sun will rise."
-Victor Hugo

I know some days you may feel used, laid out to dry, broken, unwanted and unlovable. You may feel like you've been tainted by the hurt and the pain, and you're no good. Like you're no good to the world. Like you're no good for others. Like you're no good for yourself. Let me tell you something; if you ever spend one moment thinking any of that— thinking about giving up-- stop. Write this down. On your paper. On your hand. On your heart. Anywhere you can write it so you'll see it, and you'll learn it, and you'll read it enough times that you just might start to believe it: no matter what depth of despair you find yourself in, you are never alone. No matter how deep your sorrow, there is always hope to keep you holding on. No matter how isolated you feel, there is always a reason to take the next step, the next breath, the next moment, and the next and the next. Are you believing any of these lies about your worth— maybe feeling like you are now damaged due to loss and grief, or believing that there is no good that could possibly now come in or from your life as a result? How can you give yourself grace and how can you see the beauty within yourself today?

_____

_____

_____

•••

•••

•••

•••

•●•

Prompt 12:

ANGER

"Anything that's human is mentionable, and anything that is mentionable can be more manageable. When we can talk about our feelings, they become less overwhelming, less upsetting, and less scary. The people we trust with that important talk can help us know that we are not alone."
-Fred Rogers

A common mistake we make is believing that anger is wrong or that it is something to be covered up. I remember being told by a counselor that feeling anger wasn't wrong. In fact, I should allow myself to feel it, to move through it, and to truly, deeply acknowledge it. That was the only way I could work through it. The problem was acting out in my anger, and not experiencing the feeling. How can you be honest with yourself today? Where is anger present within your heart? How can you allow yourself to feel it today, to acknowledge it and move through it?

_____

_____

_____

_____

_____

•••

•••

•••

•••

•••

Prompt 13:

DON'T FAKE IT

"While grief is fresh, every attempt to divert only irritates.
You must wait till it be digested, and then amusement
will dissipate the remains of it."
-Samuel Johnson

I know there is pressure to be more, but please don't plaster on smiles. Please don't just say the right words, go through all the right steps, letting the world choreograph your life. Please don't be afraid to be honest. Please don't cover up the hurt and suffer quietly, silently. That's not the way to mend. Healing doesn't happen under a facade, and you've been through too much to have to fake it. You need to know this: you don't have to be strong, or put together, or happy, or anything. You just need to allow your heart room to be splayed open enough to mend. Have you felt pressure to put on a face? Where has this come from? How has it made you feel? What would happen if you gave yourself permission to be yourself?

_____

_____

_____

_____

_____

•••

•••

•••

•••

Prompt 14:

LOVE LETTERS

"Yesterday, I was clever, so I wanted to change the world.
Today, I am wise, so I am changing myself."
-Rumi

    Write yourself a letter below as if your loved one were writing it to you. What would they say to you? How would they encourage you? How does it feel to imagine them and their love for you? What would they want you to let go of? What dreams do you think they'd want you to chase?

_____

_____

_____

_____

_____

_____

_____

_____

_____

•••

•••

•••

●●●

•••

Prompt 15:

COMPOUNDED GRIEF

"Grief is like a long valley, a winding valley where any bend may reveal a totally new landscape."
- CS Lewis

You've been through one of the worst experiences. Maybe you've found yourself being hit from every side, and every time you've tried to stand, one more thing comes in and pummels you into the ground. Unfortunately, compounded grief is common, and life doesn't seem to discriminate on who it hits. The important thing to remember is this: you are never alone. Have you experienced compounded grief? Have you had anyone to journey through this with you? What can you do to remind yourself that no matter how hard life gets, you are never alone?

_____

_____

_____

_____

_____

_____

_____

•••

•••

•••

•••

Prompt 16:

EXPLAINING GRIEF

"The reality is that you will grieve forever. You will not 'get over' the loss of a loved one; you will learn to live with it. You will heal and you will rebuild yourself around the loss you have suffered. You will be whole again but you will never be the same. Nor should you be the same nor would you want to."
-Elisabeth Kübler-Ross

Complete this prompt today: "I really wish others understood this…"

_____

_____

_____

_____

_____

_____

_____

_____

_____

_____

•••

•••

•••

•••

GIVING YOURSELF PERMISSION

"Grief is not a disorder, a disease or a sign of weakness.
It is an emotional, physical and spiritual necessity,
the price you pay for love. The only cure for grief is to grieve."
-Earl Grollman

Hear this today: Give yourself permission. Give yourself permission to feel. Give yourself permission to love. Give yourself permission to ache. Give yourself permission to live. They would want that. They would want the best for you. They would want you to live fully. They would want you to love deeply. They would want you to laugh. They would want you to change this world with love. They would want you to give that love to others, because they know the power of it. You— the one who will never stop saying their name. You— the one who is braving each day, putting one foot in front of the other, and living, even when part of you is worlds apart. You— the one who loves them, endlessly. You— you're still standing. You— you're still breathing. You— you're making them proud. Where do you need to give yourself permission in this season? Do you need permission to mourn? Do you need permission to live fully? Do you need permission to allow your heart to love again? What would happen if you gave yourself permission and what would that look like? How would it feel?

_____

_____

_____

•••

●●●

•••

•••

•••

Prompt 18:

VALIDATION

"So often we try to make other people feel better by minimizing their pain, by telling them that it will get better (which it will) or that there are worse things in the world (which there are). But that's not what I actually needed. What I actually needed was for someone to tell me that it hurt because it mattered."
-John Green

Write a letter to yourself today, validating your grief, validating your love for your loved one, and validating your embarkment into truly living again.what would that look like? How would it feel?

_____

_____

_____

_____

_____

_____

_____

_____

•••

•••

●●●

•••

HURTING PLACES

"Tears are words that need to be written."
-Paulo Coelho

If heartache were a physical condition and you had to describe it to someone, how would you describe the way your heart feels from the moment your loved one passed to now?

_____

_____

_____

_____

_____

_____

_____

_____

_____

_____

_____

_____

•••

•••

‎ ‎

•••

•••

LETTING GO OF GUILT

"Guilt is perhaps the most painful companion to death."
-Elisabeth Kubler-Ross

Guilt gnaws away at your very core and roots into your heart with the lie that you are somehow to blame. What if I had done more? Said more? Been more? When left unaddressed, the guilt can swallow you whole and weigh you down with shame. Relief comes when we surrender the burdens that we carry. What guilt are you holding on to? What lies have you allowed yourself to believe regarding your involvement in this tragedy? What burdens do you need to lay down today?

_____

_____

_____

_____

_____

_____

_____

_____

•••

•••

•••

•••

•••

Prompt 21:

BOUNDARIES

*"Daring to set boundaries is about having the courage
to love ourselves, even when we risk disappointing others."*
-Brene Brown

One of the most difficult parts of making it through grief can be the weight and demands of others. Sometimes, the most important words you can say are "Yes" and "No". Have you said yes to things you shouldn't have? What do you need to say yes to? What do you need to say no to?

_____

_____

_____

_____

_____

_____

_____

_____

_____

•••

•••

•••

•••

Prompt 22:

SACRED STRENGTH

*"The most beautiful people we have known
are those who have known defeat, known suffering, known struggle,
known loss, and have found their way out of the depths.
These persons have an appreciation, a sensitivity and an understanding
of life that fills them with compassions, gentleness, and a
deep loving concern. Beautiful people do not just happen."*
-Elizabeth Kubler-Ross

You are worthy. You are loved. You are brave. You have purpose. You are strong, even when you feel like no one has ever been weaker. You have a heart that is worthy of giving and receiving love, no matter how many times it has been broken. You are extraordinary just as you are. You are enough. How do I know these things? Why can I say these? Because I can look into the eyes of any one of you and see it. Keep breathing. Keep fighting. Keep coming alive. Do you realize your strength? Your bravery? Your purpose? Spend some time encouraging yourself below. What "wins" have you recently had? What are you doing well? Celebrate yourself below today. You deserve it.

_____

_____

_____

_____

•••

●●●

•••

•••

Prompt 23:

IDENTIFYING FEELINGS

*"For a seed to achieve its greatest expression,
it must come completely undone. The shell cracks, its insides come out
and everything changes. To someone who doesn't understand growth,
it would look like complete destruction."*
- Cynthia Occelli

In the space below, illustrate your feelings. For help with identifying feelings, refer to the feelings list at the back of this journal.

_____

_____

_____

_____

_____

_____

_____

_____

_____

_____

•••

•••

•••

•••

Prompt 24:

ISOLATION

"I thought I was alone who suffered.
I went on top of the house, and found every house on fire."
-Baba Farid

One of the most difficult parts of grief is how isolating it feels. You feel like others couldn't possibly understand— not you, not your situation, not your pain. The darkness of grief whispers so many lies to try to make you believe you are alone, but hear this: this could not be farther from the truth. You are not alone. There are entire bands and tribes of people suffering, just like you. Many are waiting to embrace you, many are waiting for you just to reach out, and maybe, just maybe, there is someone who needs to hear your voice speak up so they can gain the courage to do the same. You are not alone. Have you experienced the isolation of grief? What does it feel like? What does it look like? What are some ways you can remind yourself that you are not alone in this? How can you speak up and reach out to others?

_____

_____

_____

_____

_____

_____

•••

•••

•••

•••

Prompt 25:

LESSONS THROUGH LOSS

"Experience: that most brutal of teachers.
But you learn, my God do you learn."
-CS Lewis

What have been some of the greatest lessons you have learned through loss? The negative ones? The positive ones? The ones you wish you would have known sooner?

_____

_____

_____

_____

_____

_____

_____

_____

_____

_____

●●●

•••

•••

•••

RELYING ON MORE THAN YOURSELF

*"Deep grief sometimes is almost like a specific location,
a coordinate on a map of time. When you are standing in that
forest of sorrow, you cannot imagine that you could ever find your
way to a better place. But if someone can assure you that they
themselves have stood in that same place, and now have moved on,
sometimes this will bring hope."*
-Elizabeth Gilbert

It's easy for me to think I can handle life on my own. When problems become complex, my tendency is to withdraw and handle things, not wanting to burden or involve others. Maybe you've been in this situation. Maybe you've never wanted help. Maybe you feel like a burden to others, or maybe you shield yourself because you've been hurt before. Maybe you believe you have to do this on your own, or maybe you have no one around you feel like you can lean on. Loneliness comes with the isolation of suffering, but it doesn't have to stay that way. We are naturally hardwired to need others, to be in community, to love and be loved. Do you have anyone in your life you can rely on? If it doesn't look like people, it could also look like your faith. If you don't, have you considered reaching out to a local support group, to a counselor, joining a group to connect with vothers? What can you do to allow others to carry your burdens with you today? What can you do to find community?

_____

_____

•••

•••

•••

•••

Prompt 27:

SILENCE

"When grief is deepest, words are fewest."
-Ann Voskamp

Take five minutes to sit in total silence today. Breathe, pray, allow your feelings to make themselves known in the stillness. When you're done, write down anything you learned.

_____

_____

_____

_____

_____

_____

_____

_____

_____

_____

•••

•••

•••

WEARY

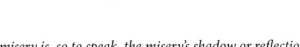

"Part of every misery is, so to speak, the misery's shadow or reflection: the fact that you don't merely suffer but have to keep on thinking about the fact that you suffer. I not only live each endless day in grief, but live each day thinking about living each day in grief."
-C. S. Lewis

I know you're weary. I can see it on your face. I can see it on the worn out, broken down look with the half smile you are trying to force. It may fool others. That's fine. No one needs to pry into your heart or try to fix you. That's not what you need. It may fool them, but it doesn't fool me, because, friend, I'm right there with you. I know you sometimes feel unappreciated when you give even though you have nothing left to give. Like all the energy you are exerting to make it through each day— to take care of others, to love with all you have— goes unnoticed. I see that, and I understand how hard it can be. Even on the days when it's hard enough to just get out of bed and plant both feet on the floor, when you can't seem to "adult" or function, it's okay. I see you. Know that some days, even just breathing is enough. Give yourself grace. Give yourself freedom. How can you give yourself more of that today? How can you take care of you— your body, your soul, your heart, your mind?

_____

_____

_____

•••

•••

•••

•••

Prompt 29:

STUBBORN HOPE

"Hope begins in the dark, the stubborn hope that if you just show up and try to do the right thing, the dawn will come. You wait and watch and work: you don't give up."
-Anne Lamott

What is hope to you? What does it look like? How can you cling to it today?

_____

_____

_____

_____

_____

_____

_____

_____

_____

_____

•••

•●•

•••

●●●

Prompt 30:

ACCEPTANCE

*"Nobody will protect you from your suffering. You can't cry it away
or eat it away or starve it away or walk it away or punch it away
or even therapy it away. It's just there, and you have to survive it.
You have to endure it. You have to live through it and love it
and move on and be better for it and run as far as you can
in the direction of your best and happiest dreams across the bridge
that was built by your own desire to heal."*
-Cheryl Strayed

Complete this prompt today, "The things I have needed to accept
since the loss of my loved one are…"

_____

_____

_____

_____

_____

_____

_____

_____

●●●

•••

•••

•••

Prompt 31:

PURPOSE

"The two most important days in your life are the day you are born, and the day you find out why."
-Mark Twain

In the darkness of grief, it's so easy to believe that there could no longer be purpose in this life. Your loved one is no longer getting their chance to live, so why should you? But the truth is this: there is still purpose, not necessarily because of the pain, but in spite of it. Love and hope are defiant forces that can arise despite all odds. They can do that in a frayed and wild mess of a life like mine, and they can do it in yours. Do you believe that you still have purpose here? If so, what does that purpose look like? Spend some time thinking about this and journaling what that might look like. Maybe this looks like prayer or maybe it's meditation or heart-searching. Turn to that and see what it is you can do to find your purpose in spite of the pain.

_____

_____

_____

_____

_____

_____

•••

•••

•••

•••

•••

Prompt 32:

EXPRESS YOURSELF

"Write hard and clear about what hurts."
-Ernest Hemingway

Write whatever is on your heart for ten minutes.

_____

_____

_____

_____

_____

_____

_____

_____

_____

_____

_____

•••

•••

•••

•••

•••

Prompt 33:

ON COMPARISON

"Comparison is the thief of joy."
-Theodore Roosevelt

It's easy to compare ourselves to others and want what they have— to wish for an easier life, to wish for a whole family, or to wish that all our loved ones were still here. But comparison often brings in guilt, or shame, or as Roosevelt pointed out, it can steal our joy. Where are you comparing your life to others? Is it in seeing others with "easier" lives? What would happen if you dropped all comparison and chose to look for the good instead? How can you quit allowing comparison to infringe on joy and gratefulness in your life?

_____

_____

_____

_____

_____

_____

_____

•••

•••

●●●

●●●

Prompt 34:

TALK ABOUT THEM

"Do you not know
that a man is not dead while his name is still spoken?"
-Terry Pratchett

Give yourself freedom today. Freedom to talk. Freedom to share. Freedom to laugh and cry and remember and mourn and love them openly, even in death. You have freedom to say their name, even if you never had a chance to say it to them while there was breath in their lungs. Say their name. Tell their story. Cry. Laugh. Celebrate. Hope. Let's move past the stigma that so often surrounds death and grief, and let's move on. Not from them but for them. Let's move on for our loved ones who deserve to be remembered, and let's move on from the stigma for others who will come after us, who will need us to pave the way for them to share their grief and their stories. Have you given yourself freedom to talk about your lost loved one? If not, do so today. If you have, how can you expand upon that freedom? How can you move past any stigma and keep sharing bravely and truly?

_____

_____

_____

_____

_____

•••

•••

•••

•••

GOOD FROM HEARTACHE

"I said: what about my eyes? He said: Keep them on the road.
I said: What about my passion? He said: Keep it burning. I said:
What about my heart? He said: Tell me what you hold inside it?
I said: Pain and sorrow. He said: Stay with it. The wound is the place
where the Light enters you."
-Rumi

     Given the choice to have been spared the pain and heartache, many of us still would choose naivety, an untainted perspective, and a heart that hasn't been broken in this way. But there are some things in life that we cannot change. It's a stark reality when you see that you are powerless to control the unraveling of your own life and circumstances. You may have watched as the perfect tapestry that was your life frayed into a wild mess. For me, after many, many tears and thousands of prayers, I realized I could spend the rest of my life sitting in the coiled, tangled threads, angry, jaded and bruised, or I could surrender and allow something new to be created— something good to come from the heartache. I didn't know what that would look like, but it was a start. What about you? Have you seen good come from your heartache? How can you search for it? Even tiny bits of good? Maybe it looks like a legacy. Maybe it's the impact they left on your life. What does that look like for you, and if you can't see it yet, what can you do to create it?

_____

_____

•••

•••

•••

•••

•••

Prompt 36:

INVISIBLE PIECES

*"And can it be that in a world so full and busy
the loss of one small creature makes a void so wide and so deep
that nothing but the width and depth of eternity can fill it?"*
-*Charles Dickens*

Grieving the loss of someone you love feels like carrying them around, hidden and invisible to the naked eye, but your spirit heavy with their memory and presence. You carry them with you everyday, and you will come to a point where the memory doesn't weigh you down with as much sadness— a day when their memory stamped on your heart is as normal to you as the color of your eyes, the sound of your own voice. How are you carrying them with you each day? How does it feel right now? Heavy or more like a new normal? What pieces of them do you cherish carrying with you?

_____

_____

_____

_____

_____

_____

•••

•••

•••

•••

Prompt 37:

PERSEVERING

"A diamond is a chunk of coal that did well under pressure."
-Henry Kissinger

Complete this prompt: "When I die, this is how I want to be remembered…"

_____

_____

_____

_____

_____

_____

_____

_____

_____

_____

•••

•••

•••

•••

Prompt 38:

LETTING IT CRASH

"Should you shield the valleys from the windstorms,
you would never see the beauty of their canyons."
-Elisabeth Kubler-Ross

Sometimes the only way to heal a little is to let the harsh waves of grief fall in to you. As they do, and as you face them, you break a little, surrendering and succumbing to their strength, to the places they take you, the memories, the scents, and the sounds your heart recalls. And sometimes, when the waves crash and you don't hide, something extraordinary happens. Sometimes, the water exposes your wounds and as it hits, it doesn't burn like it used to; it cleanses and heals them little by little. How can you allow the waves to crash over you? What are new parts of grief you are facing? What memories are coming into your mind? Allow yourself to sit and let grief crash over you for a moment. Write down your thoughts and feelings in the space below.

_____

_____

_____

_____

_____

•••

●●●

•••

●●●

•◐•

Prompt 39:

SADNESS

*"Only when we are brave enough to explore the darkness
will we discover the infinite power of our light."*
-Brene Brown

Sadness is something our world runs from. Happiness is placed on a high pedestal as the ultimate goal, and sadness is only a temporary stop along the way. But the truth is this: we need to experience sadness. Sadness is not weakness. Sadness is not abnormal. Sadness is healthy to feel in the great coexistence that is life— where grief and love and joy and sadness and an array of hundreds of other emotions all live, intermingled and side-by-side. Are you afraid of sadness or have you been willing to embrace it? How can you express the sadness within you today?

_____

_____

_____

_____

_____

_____

_____

•••

●●●

•••

•••

Prompt 40:

LOVE ANYWAY

"Unless you love someone, nothing else makes sense."
-EE Cummings

To love is to be vulnerable. When you have loved and lost—whether it's the loss of a person, the loss of a dream, the loss of something dear to you— you know this vulnerability. You may even know what it looks like to suddenly protect your heart, suddenly terrified of loving and living again for fear of being wrung and broken. But we know that's not the true way to live. We know that we were created for love— to love and be loved and to spread that love all around this world. Your loved one knows better than most the power of your love. Though they are physically absent, ask yourself what they would want you to do with that love of yours. How can you take that love and fill the world with it? What obstacles might you need to overcome in order to love again?

_____

_____

_____

_____

_____

_____

•••

•••

•••

•••

Prompt 41:

YOU'LL FIND THEM

"I swear to you,
there are divine things more beautiful than words can tell."
-Walt Whitman

Look for them all around you. Look for gentle reminders that you are loved. Look for peace and divine things that are greater than we could ever imagine. Where you do you seem them? Take time to think and pray about this today— about your eyes being opened to the divine things that are surrounding you. Where do you find them?

_____

_____

_____

_____

_____

_____

_____

_____

_____

•••

•••

•••

Prompt 42:

DON'T GIVE UP

"If you're going through hell, keep going."
-Winston Churchill

I know you feel weak, but remember that there is beauty in the brokenness. When you are reduced to nothing but soul, you radiate an extraordinary power. When you experience searing loss and your heart continues beating, there is strength in that. When pain whispers the hurtful lies and giving up and succumbing sounds like the best plan, find that strength, find that hope that is greater and that love that is deeper than any amount of pain, and then cling to it, and don't you dare let go. What keeps you holding on? Finish this prompt today, "I hold on because..." Don't close this journal until you write at least one reason.

_____

_____

_____

_____

_____

_____

_____

•••

•••

•••

•••

Prompt 43:

ALLOWING YOURSELF TO FEEL

◆―――――――◆●●――――――▶

"(exists no miracle mightier than this: to feel)"
-EE Cummings

Don't be afraid to feel. Feel pain, feel joy, feel love, feel anger, feel excitement or happiness. Feeling is good, and sometimes, after going through the hardest parts of life, we have to remind ourselves to stop ducking for cover, to stop wincing and grimacing, afraid to feel because we are afraid to break. If you are there, take a step today and let yourself feel something. It might be scary at first, it might hurt a little, but the whole thing about coming alive doesn't mean that you won't feel pain. It simply opens your heart to joy as well. What are your feelings right now? Take a minute to tap into them, to ask yourself how you're really doing beneath the surface and write it out below.

_____

_____

_____

_____

_____

_____

_____

●●●

•••

•••

•••

Prompt 44:

WITHIN

"Nothing can dim the light that shines from within."
-Maya Angelou

Today, journal on this: What is the light that shines within you?

_____

_____

_____

_____

_____

_____

_____

_____

_____

_____

_____

_____

•••

•••

•◐•

•••

THE WORTH YOU POSSESS

"Tell me,
what is it you plan to do with your one wild and precious life?"
-Mary Oliver

Sometimes our stories seem too bruised and battered to have anything good come from them. But this is not the truth. Even when it doesn't make sense, and even when you feel like the smallest person in the world. Even when you fee incapable and unqualified and it doesn't seem fathomable that you could make it through another day. Even when you think the world would be better off if you found a deep, dark hole to take up residence in and hide. Even when you're paralyzed by fear and unworthiness. Even in those moments, this is the story you've been given, and with it, no matter how bruised and battered it may be, you have something to offer to this world. Because when your hands are too small to hold all of the love, sometimes it overflows and spills on to others. Because when your voice is insignificant and little, sometimes it echoes off the walls. Because when your heart has been broken, sometimes it bleeds love and grace. When you feel you have nothing to offer, it's not true. I promise you. You do. Where is the good in your story? Do you believe you have worth? What do you believe you can do with your story to help others?

_____

_____

_____

_____

•••

•••

•••

•••

COMBATTING FEAR

"I knew that if I allowed fear to overtake me, my journey was doomed.
Fear, to a great extent, is born of a story we tell ourselves, and so
I chose to tell myself a different story from the one women are told.
I decided I was safe. I was strong. I was brave.
Nothing could vanquish me."
-Cheryl Strayed

    I know this life feels a little scary at times. One shoe has fallen, and you're just waiting for the other...In fact, maybe your whole life seems to be about just waiting on the other to fall, like you are caught in this half-wince, shielding yourself from one more blow, and wondering how you'll hold on if and when it hits. Fear is common, and when you've experienced suffering and trauma, fear is normal. However, it does not mean that we should allow fear to captivate us. Sometimes, the best thing we can do with fear is to name it. Name it below, and if you want to take it a step further, next to your fear, write down a truth that combats that fear that you can meditate on. care of you— your body, your soul, your heart, your mind?

_____

_____

_____

_____

_____

•••

•••

•••

•••

Prompt 47:

TOGETHER

"Birds with broken wings often try to help each other fly."
-Matt Baker

There's so much beauty in brokenness and mending. There's so much community when your soul is stripped bare and also when you find the strength to rise. While the rest of the world can feel isolating, hearing the voice of another person who is aching or who has ached just like you makes you feel just a little less alone— like maybe you aren't the only who has had to live with this unbearable pain, and maybe if they can survive and come alive, you can too. Do you have anyone traveling beside you? How does it feel to have them there? How do you wish someone would support you? Whether you do or don't, who can you travel alongside?

_____

_____

_____

_____

_____

_____

•••

•••

•••

•••

•••

Prompt 48:

LOSS OF SECURITY

"No one ever told me that grief felt so like fear."
-C.S. Lewis

Loss has a funny way of stripping us of our sense of security. The thing we so fiercely protected— our children, our spouse, our family members, our marriage— has been impacted by loss and despair. It is hard not to feel as if nothing is safe from the darkness of death. Perfect love casts out all fear. What are you most afraid of? What fears are you facing today? What are some steps that you can take to surrender these fears and find rest?

_____

_____

_____

_____

_____

_____

_____

_____

_____

_____

•••

•••

•••

•••

Prompt 49:

SHIFTING FOCUS

"She was no longer wresting with the grief, but could sit down with it as a lasting companion and make it a sharer in her thoughts."
-George Eliot

When the pain is fresh, it blares in your ears and drowns out everything else. As it quiets, little by little, you can begin to shift your focus— not just on the heartache but you can shift it to focusing on the good your loved one brought and still brings to this world and to you. Look for the beauty today. Where do you see it? How is their legacy manifesting itself in your life? How did they change you for the better?

_____

_____

_____

_____

_____

_____

_____

_____

•••

•••

•••

•••

Prompt 50:

TEARS

"There is a sacredness in tears. They are not the mark of weakness, but of power. They speak more eloquently than ten thousand tongues. They are the messengers of overwhelming grief, of deep contrition, and of unspeakable love."
-Washington Irving

It's easy to be afraid of tears when they come, but there is nothing wrong with them. You don't have to stifle them. You can let them flow out, cleansing you, and see them simply as an expression of your love. Give yourself safe outlets, whether your sorrow is expressed through tears, through art, through written word, through counseling, etc. When was the last time you cried? Where are your outlets? Where are you safe to express yourself? If you can't think of anything, how can you find or create an outlet?

_____

_____

_____

_____

_____

_____

_____

•••

•••

•••

•••

Prompt 51:

DREAMING AGAIN

"Hardships often prepare ordinary people
for an extraordinary destiny."
-CS Lewis

Complete this prompt today: "If I allowed myself to begin dreaming again, this is what I would do…"

_____

_____

_____

_____

_____

_____

_____

_____

_____

_____

_____

_____

•••

•••

•••

•••

Prompt 52:

MASKS

*"Owning our story and loving ourselves through that process
is the bravest thing we'll ever do."*
-Brene Brown

Hiding can become our go-to in the midst of grief. Grief can transform the life of the party into the person who avoids crowds, ducks away, and willingly stays home. Hiding can also happen in other ways. We can hide behind masks, believing that the world cannot handle our grief, and our conclusion is that we must cover it up. Are you wearing a mask? What does it look like? What is happening beneath your mask? Do you have any safe places to remove it?

_____

_____

_____

_____

_____

_____

_____

_____

•••

•••

•••

•••

Prompt 53:

SHARE YOUR HEART

"I did not want to kiss you goodbye. That was the trouble:
I wanted to kiss you goodnight and there's a lot of difference."
-Ernest Hemingway

Today, write a poem for your loved one.

_____

_____

_____

_____

_____

_____

_____

_____

_____

_____

_____

•••

•••

•••

Prompt 54:

FAITH

"Faith is deliberate confidence in the character of God whose ways you may not understand at the time."
-Oswald Chambers

Has your faith changed in the midst of your grief? Where did you place it before? Where do you place it now? Where would you like for it to grow?

_____

_____

_____

_____

_____

_____

_____

_____

_____

_____

_____

•••

•••

•••

DEALING WITH OTHERS

"But there is a discomfort that surrounds grief. It makes even the most well-intentioned people unsure of what to say. And so many of the freshly bereaved end up feeling even more alone."
-Meghan O'Rourke

I once heard someone say that the best advice they heard after the death of their son was this: "Choose to hear love." When people open their mouths, and it doesn't sound like love coming out, choose to hear love instead. People mean well. They want to love you. They want to understand, and when they see your heart, broken and laid waste, sometimes all the wrong words come out– or sometimes, out of fear, they say nothing at all. They may say nothing you want them to say and everything you wish they wouldn't. Most people genuinely want to scoop you into their arms and take away any pain; they just don't know how. So they stumble over words. They spit out platitudes, and then they walk away, either oblivious or kicking themselves in the face for struggling. I was once there. I'm sure you may have been, too. There was a "before" to our suffering when we did not have the words to say. And so. When it's possible, remember that when people open their mouths, and it doesn't feel like it's love coming out, choose to hear love instead. Choose to see a heart that wants to reach out, but just doesn't have the right words to say. How can you choose to hear love today? How can you forgive others for poor words they've said? Where can you extend grace? Is there anyone in your life you need to give that grace to today? And on the flip side, might there be anyone whose words you need to let go of?

●●●

•••

•••

•••

Prompt 56:

TURNING A LEAF

*"And the time came when the risk to remain tight in a bud
was more painful than the risk it took to blossom."*
-Anais Nin

The early days are the darkest— the aftermath— when the fog is thick and our eyes can barely discern what is before us. No one likes the darkness. The darkness adds no merit and no depth to the amount of love that we have. And at some point, we discover that grief doesn't have to exist only in the darkness. Grief will last as long as love does, but grief can be felt in the light. Grief can coexist with joy. Grief can be a slow, lifelong mending. Grief doesn't have to always be associated with anger and constant pain. Grief can sometimes feel more like a constant melody, sometimes loud, and sometimes the soothing tune of love that follows you through your days. Have you experienced the darkness? What does it feel like? Do you feel like you are still in it, or have you moved more into the light with your grief? What might hold you back, and what can you do to keep moving into the light?

_____

_____

_____

_____

•••

•••

•●•

•••

WHO WOULD THEY BE?

"The deep pain that is felt at the death of every friendly soul arises from the feeling that there is in every individual something which is inexpressible, peculiar to him alone, and is, therefore, absolutely and irretrievably lost."
-Arthur Schopenhauer

When we lose a loved one, we don't just lose them at the stage they were when they passed. We lose them at every stage we missed, and our hearts will forever ache with that knowledge. There's a whole crock of crap that says grief follows a method. It stays neatly in lines, clean, tame, strategic. But often times with death, there is nothing tame about it. For the rest of our lives, we'll be missing the should-haves. Grief will never be methodical or neat. And one thing I've learned from others much further along in this journey than me is grief doesn't end in this lifetime. Out of a broken, beating heart comes endless love as it ebbs and flows through the constant cycles of grief. Sometimes gentle, sometimes heavy. The reminders are always there. The love is always there, and next to it is gratefulness, an ache, and the question, "Who would they be today?" Who do you think they would be today if they were still physically present? What would they say to you? What do you think they would want for you in light of this?

_____

_____

_____

•••

•••

•••

SEARCHING FOR SIMPLE JOYS

"Joy is the simplest form of gratitude."
-Karl Barth

Living life in the aftermath is a balancing act. It's an awareness of the pain and the grief and the void, but it's also a hunt. A search to uncover every last ounce of good, of love, and of joy. What are some of the simple joys surrounding you today? How can you uncover good in this moment in your life? How can you hunt for it and also for love and joy? Name the good in your life below. Make a list below. If you struggle to name anything, go out today and do something that will bring you joy.

_____

_____

_____

_____

_____

_____

_____

•••

•••

•••

•••

Prompt 59:

WAVES OF GRIEF

*"Grief is like the ocean, it comes in waves, ebbing and flowing.
Sometimes the water is calm, and sometimes it is overwhelming.
All we can do is learn to swim"*
-Vicki Harrison

Often times, grief feels like you're in a river, waist-deep, walking against the thick and rushing current. Your legs are weak from the resistance, the miles are wearing on you, and it would be so much easier just to give in to the current and let it wash you away wherever it pleases. This is how grief and loss and devastation can feel. Every day is worth it. There is so much joy, but the basics of breathing and living and walking can take so much more effort through the heartache. Some days it's harder. Like the days when it rushes back to you. All the memories. All the moments. And just like that the current washes over. The ebbs and flows are unpredictable. The current gives no warning before it thickens. It just does, and you just have to learn to stand. And you wait. And in those moments, you search for your ways to healthily cope and to keep standing. What do you do when the currents of grief hit? What have you found helps you to cope in a healthy way? How do you stand through them?

_____

_____

_____

_____

•●•

•••

•••

●●●

Prompt 60:

THE AWKWARD MOMENTS OF GRIEF

"Life would be tragic if it weren't funny."
-Stephen Hawking

What do you say? What do you do? How do you meet new people? What do you say when people ask personal questions? How do you not cry in front of total strangers? How? Why? What? These are all questions you may ask yourself, and for all of these, there may be no answers. Grief and the aftermath have produced many awkward moments that, to those who understand, are entirely laughable. And maybe that's what we have to do in the most difficult and awkward moments of tough questions or public "ugly cry" sessions. We laugh, and we let them roll off our backs. What have been some of the most awkward moments you have had due to grief? How can you find ways to laugh at these moments (and acknowledge that they are entirely normal)?

_____

_____

_____

_____

_____

_____

•••

•••

•••

•••

Prompt 61:

FORGIVENESS

*"To forgive is to set a prisoner free
and discover that prisoner was you."*
-Lewis B. Smedes

Oftentimes, we place blame on others and ourselves for the heartache in our lives. Whether it's merited or not, forgiveness is not something that sets the other person free; it's something that sets us free. Who might you need to forgive? Is it someone else? Is it God? Is it yourself?

_____

_____

_____

_____

_____

_____

_____

_____

_____

•••

•••

•••

•••

Prompt 62:

REFRAMING MEMORIES

"Your memory is made of light."
-Pablo Neruda

When you think about your loved one who is no longer with you, the thoughts may be painful for a while. Tragedy likes to taint our view and cloud our vision. Depression and despair do a whole lot of that, too. It's easy to think back on memories, no matter how few we may hold, and to only view them through the darker lenses of grief. Mourning is healthy and necessary, but a day may come when you are able to reframe your memories. Maybe this means reframing them with gratefulness for the time you were given rather than sorrow over the time you've lost. Are you able to reframe memories at this point? What is the lens you are viewing them through? What might help you to reframe your perspective with gratefulness? Choose one memory, and practice reframing by writing it out below through the lens of gratefulness.

_____

_____

_____

_____

_____

•••

•••

●●●

•••

Prompt 63:

ON GROWING

"In any given moment we have two options:
to step forward into growth or to step back into safety."
-Abraham Maslow

Complete this prompt today: "If I could tell my former self one thing, I would say this…"

_____

_____

_____

_____

_____

_____

_____

_____

_____

_____

_____

•●•

•••

•••

•••

Prompt 64:

BOTH-ANDS

"One cannot get through life without pain...
What we can do is choose how to use the pain life presents to us."
-Bernie S. Siegel

    I hate cliches and trite phrases and answers that feel like pathetic pats on the back. But sometimes things are a both-and. Sometimes the circumstances we are handed can simultaneously bring misery and also reveal joy. They can bring great grief and pain, but also fill us to overflowing with a love that doesn't waver or fail. They can strip us of all we have, and then they can rebuild us, piece by piece as more compassionate, (sometimes more gritty), kinder, more gracious humans. Time is opening my eyes, and the things that once simply looked like pain-- I'm seeing that they are also a both-and. They are gifts. They can be so much more. What are some of your both-ands? List them below.

_____

_____

_____

_____

_____

_____

•••

•••

•••

•••

Prompt 65:

GRIEF IS JUST A PART OF YOU, NOT ALL OF YOU

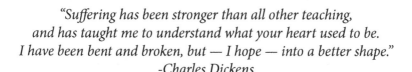

"Suffering has been stronger than all other teaching,
and has taught me to understand what your heart used to be.
I have been bent and broken, but — I hope — into a better shape."
-Charles Dickens

Loss happens. It's devastating, and sometimes you lose someone or something that can never, ever, ever be replaced. Sometimes it feels more like an amputation. Grief comes in full force, but it's still only a part of you. It doesn't steal your identity. It doesn't steal you. It sits on you like a fog, and it may change you in many ways, but beneath the grief, you're still you— changed, but still you. When you look at your life and your future, this can be one of the most defining realizations you have— your life may be crushed, but it is not over. Your heart may be broken, but it is still beating. You still have purpose. Who are you? Today, take time to describe who you are— reminding yourself of your qualities and introducing yourself to pieces that make up the "new you"— not the former person, the one who's been erased, but the one that has been stripped bare and is being built up again as a refined soul.

_____

_____

_____

_____

•••

•••

•••

•••

Prompt 66:

INTENTION

"The world is indeed full of peril, and in it there are many dark places but still there is much that is fair, and though in all the lands love is now mingled with grief, it grows perhaps the greater."
-J.R.R. Tolkien

When you've lived in survival mode post trauma and post loss, it's sometimes difficult to lift yourself out of that and back into an intentional life. Sometimes, that's even the last thing you want to do. But if you start small, taking little steps, you can move out of simply surviving and into a life of intention. What is one goal you can set for yourself right now? What is one word you can choose for your next month to strive for?

_____

_____

_____

_____

_____

_____

_____

_____

●●●

•••

•••

•••

Prompt 67:

REFUSING TO BE HARDENED

←————————————•••————————→

"Allow beauty to shatter you regularly.
The loveliest people are the ones who have been burnt and broken
and torn at the seams yet still send their open hearts into the world
to mend with love again, and again, and again. You must allow
yourself to feel your life while you're in it."
-Victoria Erickson

It's so easy to take a posture of self-protection after suffering, to shut down and shut the world out. The difficult task is this: to not let this world harden you. It will wreck you. It will break you, but when— not if— you break, remember that you don't have to harden. You don't have to let all the shattered pieces stay rough and jagged. You don't have to close off, covering your eyes, shutting down to all the bad, and consequently, all the good. You can break, and you can keep loving. You can break, and you can keep breathing. You can break, and you can resist the urge to turn away from it all, and you can uncover your eyes, rest your hands, no longer shielding and no longer pushing. And slowly, you can mend. What are your defense mechanisms you employ so that you don't allow hurt into your life? How do you self-protect? How can you allow yourself to not harden, or to become soft once again? Do you believe it's more worthy to live softly and risk pain than to live with a hardened, shut down heart?

_____

_____

_____

•••

●●●

•••

●●●

Prompt 68:

YOUR REASON

*"The sun is a daily reminder t
hat we too can rise again from the darkness,
that we too can shine our light."*
-S. Ajna

I've learned that there's a funny thing about being crushed. When your dreams have shattered, and you lose it all, you find what keeps you going. When you're stripped bare, you find a strength that is at a soul level. You find the thing that keeps you taking the next breath when all reason tells you to stop. You find the true reason you live. What is your reason? What keeps you going? What brings you joy and purpose and contentment? What keeps you holding on?

_____

_____

_____

_____

_____

_____

_____

•••

•●•

●●●

•••

Prompt 69:

ONE MORE MOMENT

"I closed my eyes and spoke to you in a thousand silent ways."
-Rumi

Complete this prompt today, "If I had one more moment with my loved one, I would…"

_____

_____

_____

_____

_____

_____

_____

_____

_____

_____

_____

_____

•••

●●●

•●•

Prompt 70:

VULNERABILITY

"Vulnerability sounds like truth and feels like courage.
Truth and courage aren't always comfortable,
but they are never weakness."
-Brene Brown

It's easy to plaster on smiles. It's easy to tell little white lies and spit out 'I'm fine's.' It's easy to even fool ourselves, numbing our consciences to the pain that is beneath the surface. It's easy to do all of those things. What's difficult is to use our voices. What's difficult is to open our hearts, and put them in front of others, exposing more of our true selves, our innermost feelings, and sharing them with authenticity. It's healing for us to be honest and open with a select few, and it's healing for others to see someone else being brave, vulnerable, and taking the first step. Are you willing to be vulnerable and share your true feelings and self? Maybe this is with a friend, maybe a counselor, maybe a pastor. Who can you be vulnerable with? What does that look like for you? What are the areas of yourself you are okay with sharing with others? What are some areas of yourself you feel like you can show to no one?

_____

_____

_____

_____

●●●

•••

•••

•••

Prompt 71:

TAKE YOUR TIME

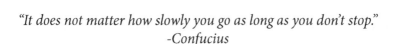

"It does not matter how slowly you go as long as you don't stop."
-Confucius

I know it feels impossible to meet the expectations and demands of life at a time when your heart is laid waste. I know. Don't let anyone rush you through your pain. There's a balance of grief and healing, of joy and brokenness, and you have to move through both to make your rough edges smooth again. You have to wade through the thick waters to heal your broken pieces, and it will happen—gradually, steadily, sometimes with setbacks, but you'll slowly mend. How can you give yourself grace? Finish this statement: "The kindest thing I can do for myself today is…?"

_____

_____

_____

_____

_____

_____

_____

•••

•●•

•••

•••

COMBATTING GUILT AND SHAME

"Shame is the intensely painful feeling
that we are unworthy of love and belonging."
-Brene Brown

The burden of guilt is far too weighty to carry, especially when you're already weary and worn down. Guilt and shame have a funny way of digging in their claws when we least expect it. I know your heart is broken. I'm so sorry it is. There truly are no words for this kind of pain, and it's not a kind that heals with only a scar. It's a lifelong wound, one that we'll brush against every day for the rest of our lives. We learn— over time— it's not as harsh. It's something that just is and always will be. But I think, given a choice, we would all choose, hands down, to feel our loved one, whether with pain or joy, for the rest of our lives than to ever wake up one day and realize that we've forgotten them entirely. So when the voice of guilt and shame becomes all you can hear, let the voice of love be louder. Where are you experiencing guilt and shame right now? There is power in naming those areas, so if you can, do so below, then next to them, answer this question: How can you allow love and light to flood into those areas? (For example: Guilt: I couldn't save him. —> Love: My job wasn't to save him; my job was to love him, and I gave him every ounce of love that I had within me, and I'll never stop.)

_____

_____

_____

•••

•••

•••

•••

Prompt 73:

PROMISES

"It is impossible for you to go on as you were before,
so you must go on as you never have."
-Cheryl Strayed

This was the promise I made to my son: I promise to find hope through the heartache, to find joy through the sadness, to find strength through incredible weakness, to love even when it's hard, to live freely and bravely, even when I'm scared, and to make the most of my days— to live in a way that would make you proud. What do you want to promise to your loved one? How can you make them proud? What can you do or are you doing?

_____

_____

_____

_____

_____

_____

_____

_____

•••

•••

•••

•••

Prompt 74:

NEVER ALONE

"They tried to bury us. They didn't know we were seeds."
-Mexican Proverb

Grief makes you feel isolated, but really, you are never grieving alone. The big thing that I needed to know is this: so many have gone before me, so many are beside me, and so many will come after me. I will never be alone. I'll never be alone in the horrible pain and loss, and I'll never be alone in the surviving. If others could survive, I could survive. If others could stay sane, I could stay sane. If others could still hope and laugh and love and live fully, then you better believe I will, too. Do you have others surrounding you— real examples of real people who have known real suffering and who are standing through it? Maybe others who have already been through the darkest moments and have made it into the light? Who gives you hope? Who makes you feel less alone? Maybe it's a friend, a relative, or maybe it's even an author or public figure whose story has resonated with you. You are never alone. Remind yourself of that today.

_____

_____

_____

_____

_____

•••

•••

•••

•••

Prompt 75:

GRATITUDE

←———————•—•———————→

"Keep your heart in wonder at the daily miracles of your life."
-Kahlil Gibran

Gratitude is often a conscious shift in our minds— lifting us from the darkness and gently opening our eyes to the light. The funny thing about gratefulness is that it likes to bleed into other areas. Start small, and your attitude will evolve before you even realize what is happening. Allow it to enter in to one area, and it can take over. You can start small. Maybe it's noticing a gentle breeze that kisses your cheek. Maybe it's a deep breath that fills your lungs like they haven't been filled in a while. Maybe it's a gallon full of ice cream. Maybe it's a quiet afternoon with someone you love. Maybe it's as simple as the way the grass feels between your toes. Maybe it's a good book. When your heart is broken, it's easy to try to shield yourself from feeling anything at all— even the good. Let yourself feel, even if it's just a moment, a moment is still a start. Spend a few days, at the end of the day, reflecting on what brought you joy that day— what you were grateful for. Even on a day when everything seems to go wrong, look for the small light. Write it down. Sometimes, you might surprise yourself, and you'll see that there were far more moments of light than you had realized. The first step is noticing them. I challenge you to write out a daily list for the next seven days. It could be a list on a piece of paper that you add to, or it could be a notebook you reserve specifically for the purpose of practicing gratefulness. What are the areas of your life that you are grateful for? What can you be grateful for today? How can you begin a practice of gratitude in your life?

•••

•••

•••

•••

LOVE FOR YOURSELF

"To love oneself is the beginning of a life-long romance."
-Oscar Wilde

It took me a good while to realize that in order to truly begin mending, I needed to have love and respect for myself. I had been at the bottom of my list, and adding any value to how I saw myself seemed insignificant. At some point, I finally realized I needed to make peace with myself, become my own friend, to extend kindness and grace to myself. I realized that I could truly begin taking steps toward bending my broken heart. Today, do something a little different. Write a letter to yourself and pretend you are a loving friend. What would you say to yourself? What would you commend yourself on? How would you see yourself through the lens of love, kindness, and grace?

_____

_____

_____

_____

_____

_____

•••

•••

•••

•••

Prompt 77:

BELIEFS

"I believe that imagination is stronger than knowledge.
That myth is more potent than history.
That dreams are more powerful than facts.
That hope always triumphs over experience.
That laughter is the only cure for grief.
And I believe that love is stronger than death."
-Robert Fulghum

Grief can challenge, strengthen, and shatter our core beliefs. How has grief influenced your beliefs? Where are the gray areas you want to seek clarity in?

_____

_____

_____

_____

_____

_____

_____

_____

•••

•••

•••

●●●

Prompt 78:

FRIENDSHIP THROUGH GRIEF

*"The friend who can be silent with us in a moment of despair
or confusion, who can stay with us in an hour of grief and
bereavement, who can tolerate not knowing... not healing, not curing...
that is a friend who cares."*
-Henri Nouwen

Grief seems to either strengthen or wither away our friendships. Even the ones that stay stagnant seem to buckle under the weight of sorrow. What has loss revealed in your friendships? Who are your safe places? Have you created any new bonds through your grief? If not, what can you do to pursue those?

_____

_____

_____

_____

_____

_____

_____

_____

•●•

•••

•••

●●●

Prompt 79:

OPEN HEARTS

◀━━━━━━━━━━◆●●━━━━━━━━━▶

"Grief can be the garden of compassion.
If you keep your heart open through everything, your pain can become
your greatest ally in your life's search for love and wisdom."
-Rumi

     The constant temptation I have is to shelter my own heart from pain, to hide away and close off to prevent any more burden being placed upon me. There have been times when my only prayer has been, "Please not one more thing." I didn't think I could take it, and my preference was to numb myself rather than endure the pain. In counseling, I learned that the best thing I could do— when I was ready— was to allow myself to feel once again, to open my heart and surrender to the healing. Where are you at in the process? What are you feeling?

_____

_____

_____

_____

_____

_____

_____

●●●

•••

•••

•••

Prompt 80:

SCARS

"You are so brave and quiet, I forget you are suffering."
-Ernest Hemingway

It only takes but a moment to be reminded of all my scars. I relive theIt only takes but a moment to be reminded of all my scars. I relive them throughout each day, tracing the lines with my fingertips, no longer wincing as much as I did in the beginning. Heartache can be to my detriment. I realize that. It could rip my life apart. Or I can sit. Firm yet still. Decided yet open to the mending. Scars covering every visible piece, but a heart that is slowly being stitched together, as painful as the process may be. I don't want to allow this heartache to be to my detriment. Never. Because I'm determined to allow the only marks he left me with to be ones of love, of beauty, of goodness. I refuse anything less. It can look like compassion for the hurting. Hope in the darkest times. Faith that is messy and unbridled. A heart that is open enough to give love. My scars may line every edge of my heart, but the story they tell will not be one purely of pain. The greater story will be that of love. A love that lasts in spite of death, a love that sets me free, a love worth living for. What is the story your scars tell?

_____

_____

_____

_____

• • •

•••

•••

•••

Prompt 81:

REJECTING STIGMA

"Let's tell the truth to people. When people ask, 'How are you?'
have the nerve sometimes to answer truthfully. You must know,
however, that people will start avaoiding you because, they, too, have
knees that pain them and heads that hurt and they don't want to know
about yours. But think of it this way: If people avoid you, you will have
more time to meditate and do fine research on a cure for whatever
truly afflicts you."
-Maya Angelou

   Grief doesn't need to be experienced silently, especially when
the silence is fueled by stigma and shame. Acknowledging your
loved one is more important than the discomfort of acquaintances.
It's healing for you— your heart— that demands to be expressed,
and it's important because of your loved one— they deserve to be
remembered. Even if society places stigma around grief, give yourself
freedom to proceed anyway. Live anyway. Express your heart anyway.
Remember them and talk about them and acknowledge them anyway. After all, you're going to love them anyway. Have you sensed any
stigma? How can you move past that a little more today? How can
you give yourself freedom to talk about them?

_____

_____

_____

_____

•••

•••

•••

•••

Prompt 82:

GAINING COURAGE

"A ship in a port is safe, but that's not what ships are built for."
-William G.T. Shedd

Complete this prompt today: "If I didn't have any insecurities or fears, I would…"

_____

_____

_____

_____

_____

_____

_____

_____

_____

_____

_____

_____

•••

•••

•••

•••

Prompt 83:

IT'S OKAY

"Sorrow makes us all children again -
destroys all differences of intellect. The wisest know nothing."
-Ralph Waldo Emerson

It's okay. It's okay to miss them. It's okay to say their name. It's okay to cry. It's okay to laugh. It's okay to breathe deeply. It's okay to smile when you think of them. It's okay to function. It's okay to have days where you can't function. It's okay to be angry. It's okay to be thankful. It's okay to love again. It's okay to remember. It's okay to hope. It's okay to be honest. It's okay to trust again. It's okay to pray. It's okay. It's okay. It's okay. Where do you need to give yourself freedom today? Take your grief temperature. How are you really? Where do you need to allow yourself space, and where do you need to push yourself along?

_____

_____

_____

_____

_____

_____

•••

•••

•••

•••

LOOKING OUTSIDE YOURSELF

"Can I see another's woe, and not be in sorrow too?
Can I see another's grief, and not seek for kind relief?"
-William Blake

Complete this prompt: "This is how I wish someone would have helped me in the midst of my grief…" and then complete this one: "This is how I would like to help others as a result…"

_____

_____

_____

_____

_____

_____

_____

_____

_____

_____

_____

•••

•••

•••

•••

Prompt 85:

FEELINGS

"Let yourself be gutted. Let it open you. Start here."
-Cheryl Strayed

Refer to the feelings chart at the back of this journal and identify and describe every feeling currently residing within you.

_____

_____

_____

_____

_____

_____

_____

_____

_____

_____

_____

•••

•••

•••

•••

Prompt 86:

STILL

"I keep thinking about you, every few minutes, all day."
-Walt Whitman

Maybe you feel like you should be "over it" or "moved on" by now. Maybe someone in your life has even spoken these words to you and put unnecessary pressure for you to carry on. But there is a difference between choosing to lie in your grief and choosing to live, understanding that grief will be lifelong. Loving someone long after their death is a feeling I haven't quite wrapped my mind around. Because time passes, the physical things falter. Their clothes no longer hold their scent. Our hands no longer remember exactly the way it felt to touch their face. And yet, they are the thought that still crosses our minds throughout every day. They are the reason to keep running when we are too tired to stand. Theirs is still one of the names that sits on our lips, just a breath away. They are a part of us, a part that will never leave. Our memories could never erase them, not the pain of their absence nor the joy of their existence. They are within us, carried within our hearts, the undercurrent of our thoughts, the inspiration to our days. This is why we still miss them, still think of them, still love them. Have you ever felt pressure to "move on"? How do you carry their legacy— as one that propels you to love and goodness, or as one that holds you in the dark? What does it look like in your life?

_____

_____

•••

•••

•••

•••

Prompt 87:

BREAKING DOWN THE BARRIERS

"When it comes time to die,
let us not discover that we have never lived."
-Henry David Thoreau

Living after loss is terrifying, and at first, it almost feels like betrayal of the one who passed. They don't get to live, so why do we deserve the chance? These are questions we may never have the answers to, but what we do have is this: we are alive. As long as we have breath in our lungs, we have a chance to live, no matter how terrifying it may feel. How can you live a little more today? What barriers are holding you back? What do you need to move past (i.e. guilt, shame, fear, etc.) in order to make peace with living?

_____

_____

_____

_____

_____

_____

_____

_____

•••

•••

●●●

•••

Prompt 88:

A VIEW OF ETERNITY

←———— •••————→

"Death has its revelations:
the great sorrows which open the heart
open the mind as well; light comes to us with our grief.
As for me, I have faith; I believe in a future life.
How could I do otherwise? My daughter was a soul;
I saw this soul. I touched it, so to speak."
-Victor Hugo

Do you believe in eternity? In Heaven? In God? Where do you believe your loved one is? Do you believe that there could be greater things awaiting us than we could ever fathom? What do you believe? And if you aren't sure, take time to wrestle through your doubts and questions below. Don't be afraid to think, to question, to pray.

_____

_____

_____

_____

_____

_____

•••

•••

•••

•••

Prompt 89:

NEW ENDINGS

"When we deny the story, it defines us.
When we own the story, we can write a brave new ending."
-Brene Brown

Complete this prompt today, "If I could dream up any possible brave new ending, this is how I would want my life to unfold from this day forward..."

_____

_____

_____

_____

_____

_____

_____

_____

_____

•••

•••

•••

•••

Prompt 90:

MAKING PEACE WITH YOURSELF

"The real difficulty is to overcome how you think about yourself."
-Maya Angelou

Because one of the greatest obstacles to healing is making peace with yourself, today, share twenty things you love about yourself.

_____

_____

_____

_____

_____

_____

_____

_____

_____

_____

_____

•••

•••

•••

Prompt 91:

FINDING YOUR PASSION

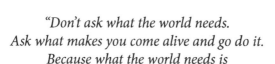

"Don't ask what the world needs.
Ask what makes you come alive and go do it.
Because what the world needs is
people who have come alive."
-Howard Thurman

For me, I had to find a way to turn his legacy into something rich, something beautiful, something beneficial to this world. The way I saw it was this: his life was far too precious to be confined to mere days, and I wanted to make sure his impact would not be bound to the same time constraints. That is when I vowed that for the rest of my life he'd be one of my greatest inspirations. What makes you come alive? Is it in a passion, a hobby, or in a dream you've never had the guts to chase? Maybe it's in beginning a foundation in honor of your loved one or doing something more to further their legacy in this world. Write some ideas down below. Brainstorm what it is that makes you come alive.

_____

_____

_____

_____

_____

•••

•••

•••

•••

Prompt 92:

FINDING FREEDOM

"You have escaped the cage. Your wings are stretched out. Now fly."
-Rumi

Complete this prompt today: "I feel the most free when…"

_____

_____

_____

_____

_____

_____

_____

_____

_____

_____

_____

_____

_____

_____

•••

•●•

•••

•••

Prompt 93:

SPEAK

"There is no greater agony than bearing an untold story inside you."
-Maya Angelou

Speak, even if no one seems to listen. Use your voice, even if you're unsure of the words. Your story, while it may be worn, tattered, messy, a little banged up and bruised, is the one you've been given. Maybe even if it doesn't make sense. Maybe even if it feels like all too much. You— your heart, your voice, your life — you matter. You have value. You have purpose, even if it's impossible to see. Embrace it, even the rough edges. All you have to do to begin is speak. Do you feel like you are speaking up and owning your story? If not, what is silencing you? Is it fear of others or of judgment? Do you know your voice has value? How can you use your voice and your story?

_____

_____

_____

_____

_____

_____

_____

•••

•••

•••

•••

Prompt 94:

EMBRACING LIFE AGAIN

"I love you with my soul because my soul never stops or forgets."
-Rumi

Embracing life again can feel a lot like you're leaving your loved one behind. Like you are moving on or letting go of their memory. But that is not the case at all. I needed to tell myself this: It's okay to love him by embracing life. It's okay if over time, the love we share looks less like heartache and more like freedom. And I also needed to tell myself this: there is no shame in that. When you choose to embrace life, you are not forgetting them. Your soul could never stop loving them or forgetting, and maybe loving them sometimes looks like finding happiness, joy, and freedom. What is holding you back? How can you embrace life today?

_____

_____

_____

_____

_____

_____

_____

●●●

•••

•••

Prompt 95:

PURSUING HEALING

"Healing is a small and ordinary and very burnt thing.
And it's one thing and one thing only:
it's doing what you have to do."
-Cheryl Strayed

Healing is in saying his name, even when it's been 21 months since my lips kissed his face. In letting the tears brim, clouding my vision, no longer holding back. Healing is standing before the mirror, and embracing every wrinkle and scar lining my young frame. Healing is surrendering, hands upturned and unfolded, laying it in His hands. Healing is splaying my heart open enough to let the oxygen hit my wounds. Healing is letting love flow into me and through me, allowing myself to both give and receive. Healing is acknowledging weakness, flaws, broken pieces. Healing is owning strengths, gifts, beauty that lies within— even the shattered parts. Healing is courage. Healing is grace— for others, for myself. Healing is love that is deeper than this world. Healing is the dry earth, bones, and the broken soil beneath my feet— mourning the pain— mourning the death— mourning the brokenness of this world, the blood that is spilled, the lives that are devalued, the cries that fill the night— mourning and crying out for salvation, for the better way it once knew. Healing sometimes comes through pain, through tears, through aches, through whispered prayers and dreams not yet seen. Healing is what I need. What you need. What we all need. Healing is love, and only that pure, unconditional love is what will pour from the sky and mend our hearts. Healing. What is healing to you? Complete this prompt today: "Healing is..."

•••

•••

•••

Prompt 96:

WHAT IF?

————————————

"Like wildflowers;
you must allow yourself to grow in all the places
people never thought you would."
E.V.

What if you gave yourself permission to grow wildly and freely? What if there were no more limitations placed on your shoulders— even by yourself? What if the purpose for your life is greater than you have yet to comprehend? What are your "What if's?"

_____

_____

_____

_____

_____

_____

_____

_____

_____

_____

•●•

•••

•••

•••

Prompt 97:

BUCKET LISTS

"You are never too old to set another goal or to dream a new dream."
-C.S. Lewis

In an effort to savor life, force yourself to create a bucket list of at least twenty items. When a loved one dies, we develop an awareness surrounding the brevity, the sacredness, and the precious nature of this life. What are twenty things you want to do before you die? Dream today, and then go out and chase those dreams. What do you have to lose?

_____

_____

_____

_____

_____

_____

_____

_____

_____

•••

•••

•••

Prompt 98:

LETTING LOVE WIN

"Unless you love someone, nothing else makes sense."
-E.E. Cummings

We can choose to say that death does not have the final say. That as long as we live, we will carry them in our hearts. And as long as our feet stand upon this dry earth, the world will still quake from the impact of their days, because that's what happens when love lives on in spite of death. Nothing is wasted. Life arises from the ashes. Redemption comes like a flood. How can you allow love to defeat death a little more today? Though the pain will still always be present in some way, how can you allow the echo of their love to ring out louder than the agony of their death?

_____

_____

_____

_____

_____

_____

_____

•••

•••

•••

•●•

Prompt 99:

WITH YOU

*"What we have once enjoyed we can never lose.
All that we love deeply becomes a part of us."*
-Helen Keller

Over time, it may feel like your loved one is more and more distant. Maybe you've forgotten their smell, their laugh, the sound of their voice. Maybe you never got to hear it at all, and you ache for it. But even as time passes, their presence that lingers cannot be erased. So we look for them. My son is with me. He's with me in my resolve because he taught me more than anyone to stand. He's with me in my love, because I learned a whole new depth of love in loving a child so much that I told him it was okay to leave. He's with me in every dream, aspiration, and goal, because he's in my very heartbeat. He's in me in my love for my older son, because he helps me to love and cherish him even more than ever before. How is your loved one with you still?

_____

_____

_____

_____

_____

_____

•••

•••

•••

•••

Prompt 100:

ON COMING ALIVE

We believe we are meant to come alive. That we, although broken, are not without value. That the most distressing of circumstances can be turned into something unconventionally beautiful. This doesn't mean we'll be without pain. This doesn't mean that we won't doubt. This doesn't mean that we'll have all the answers. This means we'll face the pain, looking it in the eye, feeling it, acknowledging it, never faking it, but embracing life for what it is, a coexistence of the deepest sorrows and the deepest joys— a vapor, to be lived with a purpose. We believe that we come alive as God begins to mend our hearts, as we reach up and reach out, grabbing on to the hands of others, grabbing on to faith, and clawing our way back to the light. We want to reach out our hands and pull one another to the light, no matter where you come from, because we don't believe that we're meant to always live in the darkness. We want to unite, no matter how different our scars may look. It doesn't matter what you've faced. It doesn't matter where you've been. We believe that no story is beyond the reach of God's grace. We believe you have inherent value, that you matter, that you are worthy and enough and entirely lovable (no matter what your broken heart may tell you). We weren't meant to do this life alone. We were meant to have each other. We see you. We see your broken, beautiful, and mending heart. We see your questions. We see your strength. We're going to take your hand, and we're going to stand in the light together. Do you believe you are coming alive? What does that look like? Compare your answer to this question to Day #1 of this journal.

_____

_____

●●‹

•••

•●•

•●•

INDEX

FEELINGS CHART

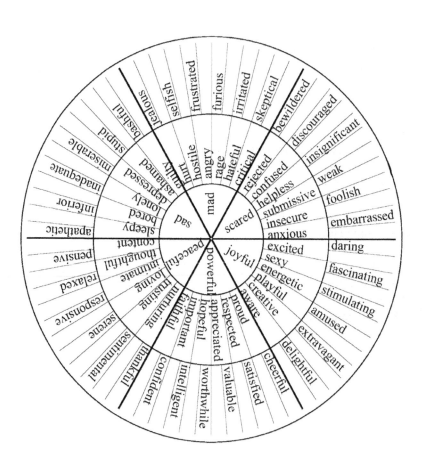

THE HEARTBEAT OF THIS JOURNAL: THE SOURCE OF HOPE

*"For I know that my redeemer lives
and at last He will stand upon the Earth."*
-Job 19:25

Dear Friend,

We know that this is the last thing you wanted. It can feel so heavy. Crushing, even. The dreams that you once had lay shattered on the floor and you are left to pick up the pieces. Maybe you feel damaged beyond repair. Broken. Worthless. Maybe you have lost all desire to keep going. Oh, friend. Do not lose hope. There is no story that is beyond the reach of God's grace. Because of Jesus, the most distressing of circumstances can be turned into something unconventionally beautiful. God stretches his arms out to us, even when we try to run. He holds us in his arms, even when we feel so far from him. He listens to our every word, even when the silence is deafening. He loves us, even when we feel shattered. You may feel angry. You may feel betrayed. You may have questions. We know. We've stood where you stand. We've shaken our fist at the heavens. We've questioned. We've doubted. We've wrestled. We've kicked and screamed and cursed. We've felt the loving arms of the Father begin to mend out hearts as we reach up and reach out, grabbed onto the hands of others, grabbing on to faith, and clawing our way back to light.

No matter what you've done, no matter where you've been, no matter what you believe, we welcome you here. It is our hope that we can come alongside one another, event at our lowest lows, and lead one another out of the darkness. This is why we do this. This is why we've created this. This is why we want to spread hope. In this, we all can find a common ground, and we all can join together, hand-in-hand.

It is about wrestling, questioning, and seeking truth together. And in this, coming alive. There is always, always hope.

So much love to you,

The On Coming Alive Team
www.oncomingalive.com